A Gift For: _____

By: _____

God's Promises® for Couples

COUNTRYMAN
®

NASHVILLE
A Thomas Nelson Company

Contents

God's Plan for Couples

God Provides for Couples

God's Guidance for Couples

God's Blessings for Couples

FAITH GOES UP THE STAIRS THAT LOVE HAS BUILT AND LOOKS OUT THE WINDOW THAT HOPE HAS OPENED.

Charles Spurgeon

God's Plan for Couples

Praying Together 🖤

This is the confidence that we have in Him, that if we ask anything according to His will, He hears us. And if we know that He hears us, whatever we ask, we know that we have the petitions that we have asked of Him.

1 John 5:14–15

Whatever you ask the Father in My name He will give you. Until now you have asked nothing in My name. Ask, and you will receive, that your joy may be full.

John 16:23–24

Whatever you bind on earth will be bound in heaven, and whatever you loose on earth will be loosed in heaven.

Matthew 18:18

It shall come to pass
That before they call, I will answer;
And while they are still speaking, I will hear.
Isaiah 65:24

Then you will call upon Me and go and pray to Me, and I will listen to you.

Jeremiah 29:12

Let us therefore come boldly to the throne of grace, that we may obtain mercy and find grace to help in time of need.

Hebrews 4:16

Cast your burden on the LORD,
And He shall sustain you;
He shall never permit the righteous to be
    moved.

Psalm 55:22

Oh, sing to the LORD a new song!
For He has done marvelous things;
His right hand and His holy arm have gained
Him the victory.

Psalm 98:1

If My people who are called by My name will humble themselves, and pray and seek My face, and turn from their wicked ways, then I will hear from heaven, and will forgive their sin and heal their land.

2 Chronicles 7:14

I love the Lord, because He has heard my voice and my supplications. Because He has inclined His ear to me, therefore I will call upon Him as long as I live.

Psalm 116:1-2

Give ear, O Lord, to my prayer; and attend to the voice of my supplications. In the day of my trouble I will call upon You, for You will answer me.

Psalm 86:6

Praising Together

Be thankful to Him, and bless His name.
For the LORD is good;
His mercy is everlasting,
And His truth endures to all generations.
Psalm 100:4–5

To Him who is able to do exceedingly abundantly above all that we ask or think, according to
the power that works in us, to Him be glory . . .
forever and ever.
Ephesians 3:20–21

I would have lost heart, unless I had believed
That I would see the goodness of the LORD
In the land of the living.
Psalm 27:13

Let us continually offer the sacrifice of praise
to God, that is, the fruit of our lips, giving thanks
to His name.
Hebrews 13:15

As for God, His way is perfect;
The word of the LORD is proven;
He is a shield to all who trust in Him.
Psalm 18:30

He is your praise, and He is your God, who has done for you these great and awesome things which your eyes have seen.

Deuteronomy 10:21

I will sing to the LORD as long as I live;
I will sing praise to my God while I have my being.

Psalm 104:33

In everything give thanks; for this is the will of God in Christ Jesus for you.

1 Thessalonians 5:18

This people I have formed for Myself; they shall declare My praise.

Isaiah 43:21

You are a chosen generation, a royal priesthood, a holy nation, His own special people, that you may proclaim the praises of Him who called you out of darkness into His marvelous light.

1 Peter 2:9

Praise the LORD!
For it is good to sing praises to our God;
For it is pleasant, and praise is beautiful.

Psalm 147:1

I will call upon the LORD, who is worthy to be praised; so shall I be saved from my enemies.

2 Samuel 22:4

I will bless the LORD at all times; His praise shall continually be in my mouth.

Psalm 34:1

Oh, clap your hands, all you peoples!
Shout to God with the voice of triumph!
Sing praises to God, sing praises!
Sing praises to our King, sing praises!
For God is the King of all the earth;
Sing praises with understanding.

Psalm 47:1, 6, 7

Whoever offers praise glorifies Me; and to him who orders his conduct aright I will show the salvation of God.

Psalm 50:23

Because Your lovingkindness is better than life,
My lips shall praise You.
Thus I will bless You while I live;
I will lift up my hands in Your name.
My soul shall be satisfied as with marrow
      and fatness,
And my mouth shall praise You with joyful lips.

Psalm 63:3–5

Great is the LORD, and greatly to be praised in the city of our God, in His holy mountain.

Psalm 48:1

It is good to give thanks to the LORD, and to sing praises to Your name, O Most High.

Psalm 92:1

The LORD is great and greatly to be praised; He is to be feared above all gods.

Psalm 96:4

Oh, that men would give thanks to the LORD for His goodness, and for His wonderful works to the children of men!

Psalm 107:8

Let my mouth be filled with Your praise
And with Your glory all the day.
But I will hope continually,
And will praise You yet more and more.

Psalm 71:8, 14

Serving God Together 🖤

How beautiful upon the mountains
Are the feet of him who brings good news,
Who proclaims peace,
Who brings glad tidings of good things,
Who proclaims salvation,
Who says to Zion,
"Your God reigns!"

Isaiah 52:7

If anyone is in Christ, he is a new creation; old things have passed away; behold, all things have become new.

2 Corinthians 5:17

I am the vine, you are the branches. He who abides in Me, and I in him, bears much fruit; for without Me you can do nothing.

John 15:5

You shall walk after the LORD your God and fear Him, and keep His commandments and obey His voice, and you shall serve Him and hold fast to Him.

Deuteronomy 13:4

Serve the LORD with gladness; come before His presence with singing.

Psalm 100:2

Then Jesus said to him, "Away with you, Satan! For it is written, 'You shall worship the LORD your God, and Him only you shall serve.'"

Matthew 4:10

No one can serve two masters; for either he will hate the one and love the other, or else he will be loyal to the one and despise the other. You cannot serve God and mammon.

Matthew 6:24

Take careful heed to do the commandment and the law which Moses the servant of the LORD commanded you, to love the LORD your God, to walk in all His ways, to keep His commandments, to hold fast to Him, and to serve Him with all your heart and with all your soul.

Joshua 22:5

I beseech you therefore, brethren, by the mercies of God, that you present your bodies a living sacrifice, holy, acceptable to God, which is your reasonable service.

And do not be conformed to this world, but be transformed by the renewing of your mind, that you may prove what is that good and acceptable and perfect will of God.

Romans 12:1–2

Be kindly affectionate to one another with brotherly love, in honor giving preference to one another; not lagging in diligence, fervent in spirit, serving the Lord; . . . distributing to the needs of the saints, given to hospitality.

Romans 12:10–11, 13

You shall serve the LORD your God, and He will bless your bread and your water. And I will take sickness away from the midst of you.

No one shall suffer miscarriage or be barren in your land; I will fulfill the number of your days.

Exodus 23:25–26

It shall be that if you earnestly obey My commandments which I command you today, to love the LORD your God and serve Him with all your heart and with all your soul, then I will give you the rain for your land in its season, the early rain and the latter rain, that you may gather in your grain, your new wine, and your oil.

And I will send grass in your fields for your livestock, that you may eat and be filled.

Deuteronomy 11:13–15

Choose for yourselves this day whom you will serve, whether the gods which your fathers served that were on the other side of the River, or the gods of the Amorites, in whose land you dwell. But as for me and my house, we will serve the LORD.

Joshua 24:15

What does the LORD your God require of you, but to fear the LORD your God, to walk in all His ways and to love Him, to serve the LORD your God with all your heart and with all your soul.

Deuteronomy 10:12

Obeying God Together 🖤🖤

Behold, I set before you today a blessing and a curse: the blessing, if you obey the commandments of the LORD your God which I command you today; and the curse, if you do not obey the commandments of the LORD your God, but turn aside from the way which I command you today, to go after other gods which you have not known.

Deuteronomy 11:26–28

Then Samuel said: "Has the LORD as great delight in burnt offerings and sacrifices, as in obeying the voice of the LORD? Behold, to obey is better than sacrifice, and to heed than the fat of rams.

1 Samuel 15:22

Oh, that you had heeded My commandments!
Then your peace would have been like a
  river,
And your righteousness like the waves of the
  sea.

Isaiah 48:18

Peter and the other apostles answered and said: "We ought to obey God rather than men.

Acts 5:29

But this is what I commanded them, saying, "Obey My voice, and I will be your God, and you shall be My people. And walk in all the ways that I have commanded you, that it may be well with you."

Jeremiah 7:23

If you love Me, keep My commandments.

He who has My commandments and keeps them, it is he who loves Me. And he who loves Me will be loved by My Father, and I will love him and manifest Myself to him.

John 14:15, 21

Now by this we know that we know Him, if we keep His commandments.

He who says, "I know Him," and does not keep His commandments, is a liar, and the truth is not in him.

But whoever keeps His word, truly the love of God is perfected in him. By this we know that we are in Him.

He who says he abides in Him ought himself also to walk just as He walked.

1 John 2:3–6

So if you walk in My ways, to keep My statutes and My commandments, as your father David walked, then I will lengthen your days.

1 Kings 3:14

And Moses called all Israel, and said to them: "Hear, O Israel, the statutes and judgments which I speak in your hearing today, that you may learn them and be careful to observe them.

"Therefore you shall be careful to do as the LORD your God has commanded you; you shall not turn aside to the right hand or to the left.

"You shall walk in all the ways which the LORD your God has commanded you, that you may live and that it may be well with you, and that you may prolong your days in the land which you shall possess.

Deuteronomy 5:1, 32, 33

Teach me to do Your will,
For You are my God;
Your Spirit is good.
Lead me in the land of uprightness.

Psalm 143:10

Drawing Closer to God Together

I have loved you with an everlasting love;
Therefore with lovingkindness I have drawn
you.

Jeremiah 31:3

Let the wicked forsake his way,
And the unrighteous man his thoughts;
Let him return to the LORD,
And He will have mercy on him;
And to our God,
For He will abundantly pardon.

Isaiah 55:7

If anyone cleanses himself . . . , he will be a
vessel for honor, sanctified and useful for the
Master, prepared for every good work.

2 Timothy 2:21

Grow in the grace and knowledge of our
Lord and Savior Jesus Christ. To Him be the glory
both now and forever. Amen.

2 Peter 3:18

As newborn babes, desire the pure milk of
the word, that you may grow thereby, if indeed
you have tasted that the Lord is gracious.

1 Peter 2:2–3

Be diligent to present yourself approved to God, a worker who does not need to be ashamed, rightly dividing the word of truth.

2 Timothy 2:15

Therefore, leaving the discussion of the elementary principles of Christ, let us go on to perfection, not laying again the foundation of repentance from dead works and of faith toward God.

Hebrews 6:1

Who are kept by the power of God through faith for salvation ready to be revealed in the last time.

In this you greatly rejoice, though now for a little while, if need be, you have been grieved by various trials, that the genuineness of your faith, being much more precious than gold that perishes, though it is tested by fire, may be found to praise, honor, and glory at the revelation of Jesus Christ, whom having not seen you love. Though now you do not see Him, yet believing, you rejoice with joy inexpressible and full of glory.

1 Peter 1:5–8

For this reason I bow my knees to the Father of our Lord Jesus Christ, from whom the whole family in heaven and earth is named, that He would grant you, according to the riches of His glory, to be strengthened with might through His Spirit in the inner man, that Christ may dwell in your hearts through faith; that you, being rooted and grounded in love, may be able to comprehend with all the saints what is the width and length and depth and height—to know the love of Christ which passes knowledge; that you may be filled with all the fullness of God.

Ephesians 3:14–19

The righteous shall flourish like a palm tree, he shall grow like a cedar in Lebanon.

Psalm 92:12

Meditate on these things; give yourself entirely to them, that your progress may be evident to all.

1 Timothy 4:15

For this reason we also, since the day we heard it, do not cease to pray for you, and to ask that you may be filled with the knowledge of His will in all wisdom and spiritual understanding; that you may walk worthy of the Lord, fully pleasing Him, being fruitful in every good work and increasing in the knowledge of God; strengthened with all might, according to His glorious power, for all patience and longsuffering with joy.

Colossians 1:9–11

But we all, with unveiled face, beholding as in a mirror the glory of the Lord, are being transformed into the same image from glory to glory, just as by the Spirit of the Lord.

2 Corinthians 3:18

Standing Strong Together

We also glory in tribulations, knowing that tribulation produces perseverance; and perseverance, character; and character, hope. Now hope does not disappoint, because the love of God has been poured out in our hearts by the Holy Spirit who was given to us.

Romans 5:3–5

For you have need of endurance, so that after you have done the will of God, you may receive the promise:

Hebrews 10:36

Be steadfast, immovable, always abounding in the work of the Lord, knowing that your labor is not in vain in the Lord.

1 Corinthians 15:58

I can do all things through Christ who strengthens me.

Philippians 4:13

Let us not grow weary while doing good, for in due season we shall reap if we do not lose heart.

Galatians 6:9

If anyone desires to come after Me, let him deny himself, and take up his cross daily, and follow Me. For whoever desires to save his life will lose it, but whoever loses his life for My sake will save it.

Luke 9:23–24

If we endure,
We shall also reign with Him.
If we deny Him,
He also will deny us.
If we are faithless,
He remains faithful;
He cannot deny Himself.

2 Timothy 2:12–13

Following God's Word Together

My son, do not forget my law,
But let your heart keep my commands;
For length of days and long life
And peace they will add to you.

Proverbs 3:1–2

Great peace have those who love Your law,
And nothing causes them to stumble.

Psalm 119:165

But he who looks into the perfect law of liberty and continues in it, and is not a forgetful hearer but a doer of the work, this one will be blessed in what he does.

James 1:25

Let the word of Christ dwell in you richly in all wisdom, teaching and admonishing one another in psalms and hymns and spiritual songs, singing with grace in your hearts to the Lord.

Colossians 3:16

If anyone desires to come after Me, let him deny himself, and take up his cross daily, and follow Me. For whoever desires to save his life will lose it, but whoever loses his life for My sake will save it.

Luke 9:23–24

Let us not grow weary while doing good, for in due season we shall reap if we do not lose heart.

Galatians 6:9

Through Your precepts I get understanding; Therefore I hate every false way.

Psalm 119:104

Supporting God's Work Together

Will a man rob God?
Yet you have robbed Me!
Bring all the tithes into the storehouse,
That there may be food in My house,
And try Me now in this,
Says the LORD of hosts,
If I will not open for you the windows of
   heaven
And pour out for you such blessing
That there will not be room enough to
   receive it.
And I will rebuke the devourer for your
   sakes,
So that he will not destroy the fruit of your
   ground,
Nor shall the vine fail to bear fruit for you in
   the field.

Malachi 3:8, 10–11

Beloved, I pray that you may prosper in all
things and be in health, just as your soul prospers.

3 John 2

But this I say: He who sows sparingly will also reap sparingly, and he who sows bountifully will also reap bountifully.

So let each one give as he purposes in his heart, not grudgingly or of necessity; for God loves a cheerful giver.

And God is able to make all grace abound toward you, that you, always having all sufficiency in all things, may have an abundance for every good work.

2 Corinthians 9:6–8

Whatever you do, do it heartily, as to the Lord and not to men, knowing that from the Lord you will receive the reward of the inheritance; for you serve the Lord Christ.

Colossians 3:23–24

Lay up for yourselves treasures in heaven, where neither moth nor rust destroys and where thieves do not break in and steal.

For where your treasure is, there your heart will be also.

Matthew 6:20–21

But seek first the kingdom of God and His righteousness, and all these things shall be added to you.

Matthew 6:33

Now concerning the collection for the saints, as I have given orders to the churches of Galatia, so you must do also: On the first day of the week let each one of you lay something aside, storing up as he may prosper, that there be no collections when I come.

1 Corinthians 16:1–2

Give, and it will be given to you: good measure, pressed down, shaken together, and running over will be put into your bosom. For with the same measure that you use, it will be measured back to you.

Luke 6:38

God Provides for Couples

Material Goods

My God shall supply all your need according to His riches in glory by Christ Jesus.

Philippians 4:19

The young lions lack and suffer hunger; but those who seek the LORD shall not lack any good thing.

Psalm 34:10

Do not worry, saying, "What shall we eat?" or "What shall we drink?" or "What shall we wear?"

For after all these things the Gentiles seek. For your heavenly Father knows that you need all these things.

But seek first the kingdom of God and His righteousness, and all these things shall be added to you.

Matthew 6:31–33

The LORD is my shepherd; I shall not want.

Psalm 23:1

The LORD will grant you plenty of goods, in the fruit of your body, in the increase of your livestock, and in the produce of your ground, in the land of which the LORD swore to your fathers to give you.

The LORD will open to you His good treasure, the heavens, to give the rain to your land in its season, and to bless all the work of your hand. You shall lend to many nations, but you shall not borrow.

Deuteronomy 28:11–12

God is able to make all grace abound toward you, that you, always having all sufficiency in all things, may have an abundance for every good work.

2 Corinthians 9:8

I have been young, and now am old; yet I have not seen the righteous forsaken, nor his descendants begging bread.

Psalm 37:25

Health

The LORD will guide you continually,
And satisfy your soul in drought,
And strengthen your bones;
You shall be like a watered garden,
And like a spring of water, whose waters do
not fail.

Isaiah 58:11

Do not be wise in your own eyes;
Fear the LORD and depart from evil.
It will be health to your flesh,
And strength to your bones.

Proverbs 3:7–8

Is anyone among you sick? Let him call for the elders of the church, and let them pray over him, anointing him with oil in the name of the Lord.

And the prayer of faith will save the sick, and the Lord will raise him up. And if he has committed sins, he will be forgiven.

James 5:14–15

You will keep him in perfect peace,
Whose mind is stayed on You,
Because he trusts in You.
Trust in the LORD forever,
For in YAH, the LORD, is everlasting strength.

Isaiah 26:3–4

Heal me, O LORD, and I shall be healed; save me, and I shall be saved, for You are my praise.

Jeremiah 17:14

Who Himself bore our sins in His own body on the tree, that we, having died to sins, might live for righteousness—by whose stripes you were healed.

1 Peter 2:24

We do not look at the things which are seen, but at the things which are not seen. For the things which are seen are temporary, but the things which are not seen are eternal.

2 Corinthians 4:18

You are the God who does wonders;
You have declared Your strength among the peoples.

Psalm 77:14

For we know that if our earthly house, this tent, is destroyed, we have a building from God, a house not made with hands, eternal in the heavens.
2 Corinthians 5:1

I pray that you may prosper in all things and be in health, just as your soul prospers.
3 John 2

Protection ❦

The LORD, He is the one who goes before you. He will be with you, He will not leave you nor forsake you; do not fear nor be dismayed.

Deuteronomy 31:8

The LORD will be a shelter for His people,
And the strength of the children of Israel.

Joel 3:16

When you pass through the waters, I will be with you;
And through the rivers, they shall not overflow you.
When you walk through the fire, you shall not be burned,
Nor shall the flame scorch you.

Isaiah 43:2

He who dwells in the secret place of the Most High shall abide under the shadow of the Almighty.

Psalm 91:1

In righteousness you shall be established; you shall be far from oppression, for you shall not fear; and from terror, for it shall not come near you.

Isaiah 54:14

Do not be afraid of sudden terror,
Nor of trouble from the wicked when it comes;
For the LORD will be your confidence,
And will keep your foot from being caught.
Proverbs 3:25–26

No evil shall befall you,
Nor shall any plague come near your dwelling;
For He shall give His angels charge over you,
To keep you in all your ways.
Psalm 91:10–11

In God I have put my trust; I will not be afraid. What can man do to me?
Psalm 56:11

He shall cover you with His feathers,
And under His wings you shall take refuge;
His truth shall be your shield and buckler.
You shall not be afraid of the terror by night,
Nor of the arrow that flies by day,
Nor of the pestilence that walks in darkness,
Nor of the destruction that lays waste at
noonday.
Psalm 91:4–6

You prepare a table before me in the presence
of my enemies;
You anoint my head with oil;
My cup runs over.

Psalm 23:5

Be of good courage, and He shall strengthen
your heart, all you who hope in the LORD.

Psalm 31:24

The LORD is my light and my salvation;
Whom shall I fear?
The LORD is the strength of my life;
Of whom shall I be afraid? . . .
Though an army may encamp against me,
My heart shall not fear;
Though war should rise against me,
In this I will be confident.

Psalm 27:1, 3

We may boldly say: "The LORD is my helper;
I will not fear. What can man do to me?"

Hebrews 13:6

Strength

But those who wait on the LORD
Shall renew their strength;
They shall mount up with wings like eagles,
They shall run and not be weary,
They shall walk and not faint.

Isaiah 40:31

In returning and rest you shall be saved;
In quietness and confidence shall be your
strength.

Isaiah 30:15

My soul melts from heaviness; strengthen me
according to Your word.

Psalm 119:28

He gives power to the weak,
And to those who have no might He increases
strength.

Isaiah 40:29

Counsel is mine, and sound wisdom; I am
understanding, I have strength.

Proverbs 8:14

Finally, my brethren, be strong in the Lord and in the power of His might.

Ephesians 6:10

That He would grant you, according to the riches of His glory, to be strengthened with might through His Spirit in the inner man.

Ephesians 3:16

That you may walk worthy of the Lord, fully pleasing Him, being fruitful in every good work and increasing in the knowledge of God; strengthened with all might, according to His glorious power, for all patience and longsuffering with joy; giving thanks to the Father who has qualified us to be partakers of the inheritance of the saints in the light.

Colossians 1:10–12

Do not sorrow, for the joy of the LORD is your strength.

Nehemiah 8:10

The LORD is my rock and my fortress and my deliverer;
My God, my strength, in whom I will trust;
My shield and the horn of my salvation, my stronghold.

Psalm 18:2

Fear not, for I am with you;
Be not dismayed, for I am your God.
I will strengthen you,
Yes, I will help you,
I will uphold you with My righteous right hand.

Isaiah 41:10

The words of a wise man's mouth are gracious.

Ecclesiastes 10:12

A man will be commended according to his wisdom.

Proverbs 10:12

The wise in heart will be called prudent, and sweetness of the lips increases learning.

Proverbs 16:21

Wisdom

I will instruct you and teach you
in the way you should go; I will
guide you with My eye.

Psalm 32:8

Lean not on your own understanding;
in all your ways acknowledge Him
and He shall direct your paths.

Proverbs 3:5–6

The wisdom that is from above is first pure,
then peaceable, gentle, willing to yield, full of
mercy and good fruits, without partiality and
without hypocrisy. Now the fruit of righteousness
is sown in peace by those who make peace.

James 3:17–18

Through wisdom a house is built,
And by understanding it is established;

Proverbs 24:3

For the LORD gives wisdom;
From His mouth come knowledge and
understanding;

Proverbs 2:6

Let the word of Christ dwell in you richly in all wisdom, teaching and admonishing one another in psalms and hymns and spiritual songs, singing with grace in your hearts to the Lord.

Colossians 3:16

Therefore settle it in your hearts not to meditate beforehand on what you will answer; for I will give you a mouth and wisdom which all your adversaries will not be able to contradict or resist.

Luke 21:14–15

I have taught you in the way of wisdom;
I have led you in right paths.
When you walk, your steps will not be hindered,
And when you run, you will not stumble.
Take firm hold of instruction, do not let go;
Keep her, for she is your life.

Proverbs 4:11–13

If any of you lacks wisdom, let him ask of God, who gives to all liberally and without reproach, and it will be given to him.

James 1:5

Patience 🖤

We know that all things work together for good to those who love God, to those who are the called according to His purpose.

Romans 8:28

Therefore be patient, brethren, until the coming of the Lord. See how the farmer waits for the precious fruit of the earth, waiting patiently for it until it receives the early and latter rain. You also be patient. Establish your hearts, for the coming of the Lord is at hand.

James 5:7–8

Now no chastening seems to be joyful for the present, but painful; nevertheless, afterward it yields the peaceable fruit of righteousness to those who have been trained by it.

Hebrews 12:11

The young lions lack and suffer hunger; but those who seek the LORD shall not lack any good thing.

Psalm 34:10

Trust in the LORD, and do good; dwell in the land, and feed on His faithfulness.

Psalm 37:3

I know how to be abased, and I know how to abound. Everywhere and in all things I have learned both to be full and to be hungry, both to abound and to suffer need.

I can do all things through Christ who strengthens me.

Philippians 4:12–13

God is able to make all grace abound toward you, that you, always having all sufficiency in all things, may have an abundance for every good work.

2 Corinthians 9:8

Courage

Wait on the LORD;
Be of good courage,
And He shall strengthen your heart;
Wait, I say, on the LORD!

Psalm 27:14

Be strong and of good courage, do not fear nor be afraid of them; for the LORD your God, He is the One who goes with you. He will not leave you nor forsake you."

Deuteronomy 31:6

Have I not commanded you? Be strong and of good courage; do not be afraid, nor be dismayed, for the LORD your God is with you wherever you go.

Joshua 1:9

God is our refuge and strength, a very present help in trouble.

Psalm 46:1

The name of the LORD is a strong tower; the righteous run to it and are safe.

Proverbs 18:10

Let not your heart be troubled; you believe in God, believe also in Me.

John 14:1

Let the peace of God rule in your hearts, to which also you were called in one body; and be thankful.

Colossians 3:15

God has not given us a spirit of fear, but of power and of love and of a sound mind.

2 Timothy 1:7

Be of good courage, and He shall strengthen your heart, all you who hope in the LORD.

Psalm 31:24

Joy

> So the ransomed of the LORD shall return,
> And come to Zion with singing,
> With everlasting joy on their heads.
> They shall obtain joy and gladness;
> Sorrow and sighing shall flee away.
>
> *Isaiah 51:11*

> The righteous shall be glad in the LORD, and
> trust in Him.
> And all the upright in heart shall glory.
>
> *Psalm 64:10*

> Then our mouth was filled with laughter,
> And our tongue with singing.
> Then they said among the nations,
> "The LORD has done great things for them."
> The LORD has done great things for us,
> And we are glad.
>
> *Psalm 126:2–3*

> These things I have spoken to you, that My
> joy may remain in you, and that your joy may be
> full.
>
> *John 15:11*

Let all those rejoice who put their trust in You;

Let them ever shout for joy, because You defend them;

Let those also who love Your name
Be joyful in You.
For You, O LORD, will bless the righteous;

With favor You will surround him as with a shield.

Psalm 5:11–12

A merry heart makes a cheerful countenance, but by sorrow of the heart the spirit is broken.

Proverbs 15:13

God has not given us a spirit of fear, but of power and of love and of a sound mind.

2 Timothy 1:7

The kingdom of God is not eating and drinking, but righteousness and peace and joy in the Holy Spirit.

Romans 14:17

A merry heart does good, like medicine, but a broken spirit dries the bones.

Proverbs 17:22

You love righteousness and hate wickedness; Therefore God, Your God, has anointed You With the oil of gladness more than Your companions.

Psalm 45:7

And you became followers of us and of the Lord, having received the word in much affliction, with joy of the Holy Spirit.

1 Thessalonians 1:6

Restore to me the joy of Your salvation, And uphold me by Your generous Spirit. Then I will teach transgressors Your ways, And sinners shall be converted to You.

Psalm 51:12–13

This is the day the LORD has made; we will rejoice and be glad in it.

Psalm 118:24

But the fruit of the Spirit is love, joy, peace, longsuffering, kindness, goodness, faithfulness.

Galatians 5:22

Comfort

> To console those who mourn in Zion,
> To give them beauty for ashes,
> The oil of joy for mourning,
> The garment of praise for the spirit of heavi-
> ness;
> That they may be called trees of righteousness,
> The planting of the LORD, that He may
> be glorified.

Isaiah 61:3

Blessed be the God and Father of our Lord Jesus Christ, the Father of mercies and God of all comfort, who comforts us in all our tribulation, that we may be able to comfort those who are in any trouble, with the comfort with which we ourselves are comforted by God.

2 Corinthians 1:3–4

He heals the brokenhearted and binds up their wounds.

Psalm 147:3

If we hope for what we do not see, we eagerly wait for it with perseverance.

Romans 8:25

When you pass through the waters, I will be with you;

And through the rivers, they shall not overflow you.

When you walk through the fire, you shall not be burned,

Nor shall the flame scorch you.

Isaiah 43:2

The eternal God is your refuge, and underneath are the everlasting arms; He will thrust out the enemy from before you, and will say, "Destroy!"

Deuteronomy 33:27

It is good that one should hope and wait quietly for the salvation of the LORD.

Lamentations 3:26

Peace

Peace I leave with you, My peace I give to you; not as the world gives do I give to you. Let not your heart be troubled, neither let it be afraid.

John 14:27

The LORD will give strength to His people;
The LORD will bless His people with peace.

Psalm 29:11

For you shall go out with joy,
And be led out with peace;
The mountains and the hills
Shall break forth into singing before you,
And all the trees of the field shall clap their
hands.

Isaiah 55:12

Great peace have those who love Your law, and nothing causes them to stumble.

Psalm 119:165

God is not the author of confusion but of peace.

1 Corinthians 14:33

You will keep him in perfect peace, whose mind is stayed on You, because he trusts in You.

Isaiah 26:3

May the God of hope fill you with all joy and peace in believing, that you may abound in hope by the power of the Holy Spirit.

Romans 15:13

The wisdom that is from above is first pure, then peaceable, gentle, willing to yield, full of mercy and good fruits, without partiality and without hypocrisy. Now the fruit of righteousness is sown in peace by those who make peace.

James 3:17–18

Let the peace of God rule in your hearts, to which also you were called in one body, and be thankful.

Colossians 3:15

God has not given us a spirit of fear, but of power and of love and of a sound mind.

2 Timothy 1:7

God is our refuge and strength, a very present help in trouble. Therefore we will not fear.

Psalm 46:1

God's Guidance for Couples

Finances 🖤

And you shall remember the LORD your God, for it is He who gives you power to get wealth, that He may establish His covenant which He swore to your fathers, as it is this day.

Deuteronomy 8:18

Trust in the LORD with all your heart,
And lean not on your own understanding;
In all your ways acknowledge Him,
And He shall direct your paths.
Do not be wise in your own eyes;
Fear the LORD and depart from evil.
It will be health to your flesh,
And strength to your bones.
Honor the LORD with your possessions,
And with the firstfruits of all your increase;
So your barns will be filled with plenty,
And your vats will overflow with new wine.

Proverbs 3:5–10

Then you will prosper, if you take care to fulfill the statutes and judgments with which the LORD charged Moses concerning Israel. Be strong and of good courage; do not fear nor be dismayed.

1 Chronicles 22:13

But seek first the kingdom of God and His righteousness, and all these things shall be added to you.

Matthew 6:33

Through wisdom a house is built,
And by understanding it is established;
By knowledge the rooms are filled
With all precious and pleasant riches.

Proverbs 24:3–4

Not lagging in diligence, fervent in spirit, serving the Lord.

Romans 12:11

Masters, give your bondservants what is just and fair, knowing that you also have a Master in heaven.

Colossians 4:1

Overcoming Temptation

Blessed is the man who endures temptation; for when he has been approved, he will receive the crown of life which the Lord has promised to those who love Him.

James 1:12

The Lord knows how to deliver the godly out of temptations and to reserve the unjust under punishment for the day of judgment.

2 Peter 2:9

No temptation has overtaken you except such as is common to man; but God is faithful, who will not allow you to be tempted beyond what you are able, but with the temptation will also make the way of escape, that you may be able to bear it.

1 Corinthians 10:13

In righteousness you shall be established;
You shall be far from oppression, for you
    shall not fear;
And from terror, for it shall not come near
    you.

Isaiah 54:14

You have also given me the shield of Your
	salvation;
Your right hand has held me up,
Your gentleness has made me great.
You enlarged my path under me,
So my feet did not slip.

Psalm 18:35–36

He who dwells in the secret place of the Most
	High
Shall abide under the shadow of the Almighty.
Psalm 91:1

Knowing God's Will

This is God,
Our God forever and ever;
He will be our guide
Even to death.

Psalm 48:14

When He, the Spirit of truth, has come, He will guide you into all truth.

John 16:13

The LORD is my shepherd;
I shall not want.
He makes me to lie down in green pastures;
He leads me beside the still waters.

Psalm 23:1–2

The LORD will guide you continually,
And satisfy your soul in drought,
And strengthen your bones;
You shall be like a watered garden,
And like a spring of water, whose waters do
    not fail.

Isaiah 58:11

The spirit of a man is the lamp of the LORD, searching all the inner depths of his heart.

Proverbs 20:27

"For My thoughts are not your thoughts,
Nor are your ways My ways," says the LORD.
"For as the heavens are higher than the earth,
So are My ways higher than your ways,
And My thoughts than your thoughts."

Isaiah 55:8–9

Beloved, do not believe every spirit, but test the spirits, whether they are of God; because many false prophets have gone out into the world.

1 John 4:1

He found him in a desert land
And in the wasteland, a howling wilderness;
He encircled him, He instructed him,
He kept him as the apple of His eye.
As an eagle stirs up its nest,
Hovers over its young,
Spreading out its wings, taking them up,
Carrying them on its wings,
So the LORD alone led him.

Deuteronomy 32:10–12

So he shepherded them according to the integrity of his heart, and guided them by the skillfulness of his hands.

Psalm 78:72

You shall not go out with haste,
Nor go by flight;
For the LORD will go before you,
And the God of Israel will be your rear guard.
Isaiah 52:12

A man's heart plans his way,
But the LORD directs his steps.
The lot is cast into the lap,
But its every decision is from the LORD.
Proverbs 16:9, 33

Fellowship with Believers

Confess your trespasses to one another, and pray for one another, that you may be healed. The effective, fervent prayer of a righteous man avails much.

James 5:16

Two are better than one,
Because they have a good reward for their labor.
For if they fall, one will lift up his companion.
But woe to him who is alone when he falls,
For he has no one to help him up.

Ecclesiastes 4:9–10

If two of you agree on earth concerning anything that they ask, it will be done for them by My Father in heaven. For where two or three are gathered together in My name, I am there in the midst of them.

Matthew 18:19–20

But now God has set the members, each one of them, in the body just as He pleased.

And if they were all one member, where would the body be?

But now indeed there are many members, yet one body.

And the eye cannot say to the hand, "I have no need of you"; nor again the head to the feet, "I have no need of you."

No, much rather, those members of the body which seem to be weaker are necessary.

And those members of the body which we think to be less honorable, on these we bestow greater honor; and our unpresentable parts have greater modesty, but our presentable parts have no need. But God composed the body, having given greater honor to that part which lacks it, that there should be no schism in the body, but that the members should have the same care for one another.

And if one member suffers, all the members suffer with it; or if one member is honored, all the members rejoice with it.

Now you are the body of Christ, and members individually.

1 Corinthians 12:18–27

Let the word of Christ dwell in you richly in all wisdom, teaching and admonishing one another in psalms and hymns and spiritual songs, singing with grace in your hearts to the Lord.

Colossians 3:16

Now, therefore, you are no longer strangers and foreigners, but fellow citizens with the saints and members of the household of God, having been built on the foundation of the apostles and prophets, Jesus Christ Himself being the chief cornerstone, in whom the whole building, being joined together, grows into a holy temple in the Lord, in whom you also are being built together for a dwelling place of God in the Spirit.

Ephesians 2:19–22

All of you be of one mind, having compassion for one another; love as brothers, be tenderhearted, be courteous; not returning evil for evil or reviling for reviling, but on the contrary blessing, knowing that you were called to this, that you may inherit a blessing.

1 Peter 3:8–9

Neither he who plants is anything, nor he who waters, but God who gives the increase.

Now he who plants and he who waters are one, and each one will receive his own reward according to his own labor.

For we are God's fellow workers; you are God's field, you are God's building.

1 Corinthians 3:7–9

You call me Teacher and Lord, and you say well, for so I am.

If I then, your Lord and Teacher, have washed your feet, you also ought to wash one another's feet.

For I have given you an example, that you should do as I have done to you.

John 13:13–15

Arise, shine;
For your light has come!
And the glory of the LORD is risen upon you.
For behold, the darkness shall cover the earth,
And deep darkness the people;
But the LORD will arise over you,
And His glory will be seen upon you.

Isaiah 60:1–2

Marriage 🖤

And the LORD God said, "It is not good that man should be alone; I will make him a helper comparable to him."

Therefore a man shall leave his father and mother and be joined to his wife, and they shall become one flesh.

Genesis 2:18, 24

He who finds a wife finds a good thing, and obtains favor from the LORD.

Proverbs 18:22

Marriage is honorable among all, and the bed undefiled; but fornicators and adulterers God will judge.

Hebrews 13:4

Let each man have his own wife, and let each woman have her own husband.

Let the husband render to his wife the affection due her, and likewise also the wife to her husband.

The wife does not have authority over her own body, but the husband does. And likewise the husband does not have authority over his own body, but the wife does.

1 Corinthians 7:2–4

Wives, submit to your own husbands, as to the Lord.

For the husband is head of the wife, as also Christ is head of the church; and He is the Savior of the body.

Therefore, just as the church is subject to Christ, so let the wives be to their own husbands in everything.

Husbands, love your wives, just as Christ also loved the church and gave Himself for her, that He might sanctify and cleanse her with the washing of water by the word, that He might present her to Himself a glorious church, not having spot or wrinkle or any such thing, but that she should be holy and without blemish.

So husbands ought to love their own wives as their own bodies; he who loves his wife loves himself.

For no one ever hated his own flesh, but nourishes and cherishes it, just as the Lord does the church. For we are members of His body, of His flesh and of His bones.

Ephesians 5:22–31

Therefore I desire that the younger widows marry, bear children, manage the house, give no opportunity to the adversary to speak reproachfully.

1 Timothy 5:14

Neither is man independent of woman, nor woman independent of man, in the Lord. For as woman came from man, even so man also comes through woman.

1 Corinthians 11:11–12

This is now bone of my bones
And flesh of my flesh;
She shall be called Woman,
Because she was taken out of Man.

Genesis 2:23

Submitting to one another in the fear of God.
Ephesians 5:21

Family

Believe on the Lord Jesus Christ, and you will be saved, you and your household.

Acts 16:31

As for me and my house, we will serve the LORD.

Joshua 24:15

Let all bitterness, wrath, anger, clamor, and evil speaking be put away from you, with all malice.
And be kind to one another, tenderhearted, forgiving one another, just as God in Christ forgave you.

Ephesians 4:31–32

Train up a child in the way he should go, and when he is old he will not depart from it.

Proverbs 22:6

These words which I command you today shall be in your heart.
You shall teach them diligently to your children, and shall talk of them when you sit in your house, when you walk by the way, when you lie down, and when you rise up.

Deuteronomy 6:6–7

And he will turn
The hearts of the fathers to the children,
And the hearts of the children to their
fathers.

Malachi 4:6

Children's children are the crown of old men,
and the glory of children is their father.

Proverbs 17:6

Correct your son, and he will give you rest;
yes, he will give delight to your soul.

Proverbs 29:17

But the mercy of the LORD *is* from everlasting
to everlasting
On those who fear Him,
And His righteousness to children's children,
To such as keep His covenant,
And to those who remember His commandments to do them.

Psalm 103:17–18

The father of the righteous will greatly rejoice,
And he who begets a wise child will delight
in him.

Proverbs 23:24

Husbands 🖤

He who follows righteousness and mercy
Finds life, righteousness and honor.

Proverbs 21:21

The righteous man walks in his integrity;
His children are blessed after him.

Proverbs 20:7

Love suffers long *and* is kind; love does not
envy; love does not parade itself, is not puffed up;
does not behave rudely, does not seek its own, is
not provoked, thinks no evil; does not rejoice in
iniquity, but rejoices in the truth; bears all things,
believes all things, hopes all things, endures all
things. Love never fails.

1 Corinthians 13:4–8

Through wisdom a house is built,
And by understanding it is established;

Proverbs 24:3

For the LORD gives wisdom;
From His mouth come knowledge and
understanding.

Proverbs 2:6

A husband is not to divorce his wife.

1 Corinthians 7:10

Husbands, likewise, dwell with them with understanding, giving honor to the wife as to the weaker vessel, and as being heirs together of the grace of life, that your prayers may not be hindered.

1 Peter 3:7

Live joyfully with the wife whom you love all the days of your vain life which He has given you under the sun, all your days of vanity; for that is your portion in life, and in the labor which you perform under the sun.

Ecclesiastes 9:9

Let your fountain be blessed,
And rejoice with the wife of your youth.
As a loving deer and a graceful doe,
Let her breasts satisfy you at all times;
And always be enraptured with her love.

Proverbs 5:18–19

Wives

He who finds a wife finds a good thing, and obtains favor from the LORD.

Proverbs 18:22

Blessed is every one who fears the LORD,
Who walks in His ways.
When you eat the labor of your hands,
You shall be happy, and it shall be well
  with you.
Your wife shall be like a fruitful vine
In the very heart of your house,
Your children like olive plants
All around your table.
Behold, thus shall the man be blessed
Who fears the LORD.

Psalm 128:1–4

Wives, submit to your own husbands, as is fitting in the Lord.

Colossians 3:18

Let the husband render to his wife the affection due her, and likewise also the wife to her husband.

1 Corinthians 7:3

Wives, likewise, be submissive to your own husbands, that even if some do not obey the word, they, without a word, may be won by the conduct of their wives, when they observe your chaste conduct accompanied by fear.

Do not let your adornment be merely outward—arranging the hair, wearing gold, or putting on fine apparel—rather let it be the hidden person of the heart, with the incorruptible beauty of a gentle and quiet spirit, which is very precious in the sight of God.

For in this manner, in former times, the holy women who trusted in God also adorned themselves, being submissive to their own husbands, as Sarah obeyed Abraham, calling him lord, whose daughters you are if you do good and are not afraid with any terror.

1 Peter 3:1–6

The wise woman builds her house, but the foolish pulls it down with her hands.

Proverbs 14:1

Houses and riches are an inheritance from fathers, but a prudent wife is from the LORD.

Proverbs 19:14

A gracious woman retains honor.

Proverbs 11:16

An excellent wife is the crown of her husband.

Proverbs 12:4

God's Truths for
Couples

God—Your Heavenly Father

"I will be a Father to you,
And you shall be My sons and daughters,"
Says the LORD Almighty.

2 Corinthians 6:18

As a father pities his children,
So the LORD pities those who fear Him.

Psalm 103:13

You, O LORD, are our Father;
Our Redeemer from Everlasting is Your name.

Isaiah 63:16

He Himself has said, "I will never leave you
nor forsake you."

Hebrews 13:5

Lo, I am with you always, even to the end of
the age." Amen.

Matthew 28:20

His compassions fail not,
They are new every morning;
Great is Your faithfulness.

Lamentations 3:22–23

We love Him because He first loved us.

1 John 4:19

We have known and believed the love that God has for us. God is love, and he who abides in love abides in God, and God in him.

1 John 4:16

Jesus—Your Savior

For God so loved the world that He gave His only begotten Son, that whoever believes in Him should not perish but have everlasting life.

John 3:16

For God did not send His Son into the world to condemn the world, but that the world through Him might be saved.

John 3:17

For all have sinned and fall short of the glory of God.

Romans 3:23

But God demonstrates His own love toward us, in that while we were still sinners, Christ died for us.

Romans 5:8

For the wages of sin is death, but the gift of God is eternal life in Christ Jesus our Lord.

Romans 6:23

Therefore, just as through one man sin entered the world, and death through sin, and thus death spread to all men, because all sinned.

Romans 5:12

He who believes in the Son has everlasting life; and he who does not believe the Son shall not see life, but the wrath of God abides on him.

John 3:36

But as many as received Him, to them He gave the right to become children of God, to those who believe in His name.

John 1:12

For by grace you have been saved through faith, and that not of yourselves; it is the gift of God, not of works, lest anyone should boast.

Ephesians 2:8–9

Behold, I stand at the door and knock. If anyone hears My voice and opens the door, I will come in to him and dine with him, and he with Me.

Revelation 3:20

If you confess with your mouth the Lord Jesus and believe in your heart that God has raised Him from the dead, you will be saved.

For with the heart one believes unto righteousness, and with the mouth confession is made unto salvation.

Romans 10:8–10

And this is the testimony: that God has given us eternal life, and this life is in His Son.

He who has the Son has life; he who does not have the Son of God does not have life.

These things I have written to you who believe in the name of the Son of God, that you may know that you have eternal life, and that you may continue to believe in the name of the Son of God.

1 John 5:11–13

The Holy Spirit—Your Helper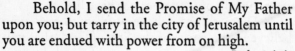

Behold, I send the Promise of My Father upon you; but tarry in the city of Jerusalem until you are endued with power from on high.

Luke 24:49

When He, the Spirit of truth, has come, He will guide you into all truth; for He will not speak on His own authority, but whatever He hears He will speak; and He will tell you things to come.

John 16:13

You shall receive power when the Holy Spirit has come upon you; and you shall be witnesses to Me in Jerusalem, and in all Judea and Samaria, and to the end of the earth.

Acts 1:8

The Holy Spirit will teach you in that very hour what you ought to say.

Luke 12:12

It is the Spirit who gives life; the flesh profits nothing. The words that I speak to you are spirit, and they are life.

John 6:63

The fruit of the Spirit is love, joy, peace, longsuffering, kindness, goodness, faithfulness, gentleness, self-control. Against such there is no law.

And those who are Christ's have crucified the flesh with its passions and desires.

If we live in the Spirit, let us also walk in the Spirit.

Galatians 5:22–25

So shall they fear
The name of the LORD from the west,
And His glory from the rising of the sun;
When the enemy comes in like a flood,
The Spirit of the LORD will lift up a standard
   against him.

Isaiah 59:19

But you, beloved, building yourselves up on your most holy faith, praying in the Holy Spirit, keep yourselves in the love of God, looking for the mercy of our Lord Jesus Christ unto eternal life.

Jude 20, 21

Who also made us sufficient as ministers of the new covenant, not of the letter but of the Spirit; for the letter kills, but the Spirit gives life.

Now the Lord is the Spirit; and where the Spirit of the Lord is, there is liberty.

But we all, with unveiled face, beholding as in a mirror the glory of the Lord, are being transformed into the same image from glory to glory, just as by the Spirit of the Lord.

2 Corinthians 3:6, 17–18

God's Word 🖤

The word of God is living and powerful, and sharper than any two-edged sword, piercing even to the division of soul and spirit, and of joints and marrow, and is a discerner of the thoughts and intents of the heart.

Hebrews 4:12

Your word I have hidden in my heart, that I might not sin against You!
I will delight myself in Your statutes; I will not forget Your word.

Psalm 119:11, 16

How sweet are Your words to my taste,
Sweeter than honey to my mouth!
Through Your precepts I get understanding;
Therefore I hate every false way.
Your word is a lamp to my feet
And a light to my path.

Psalm 119:103–105

By the word of the LORD the heavens were made, and all the host of them by the breath of His mouth.

Psalm 33:6

Forever, O LORD,
Your word is settled in heaven.
Your faithfulness endures to all generations;
You established the earth, and it abides.

Psalm 119:89–90

Your testimonies are wonderful;
Therefore my soul keeps them.
The entrance of Your words gives light;
It gives understanding to the simple.

Psalm 119:129–130

As newborn babes, desire the pure milk of the word, that you may grow thereby, if indeed you have tasted that the Lord is gracious.

1 Peter 2:2–3

You are already clean because of the word which I have spoken to you.

John 15:3

Heaven and earth will pass away, but My words will by no means pass away.

Luke 21:33

If you abide in My word, you are My disciples indeed. And you shall know the truth, and the truth shall make you free.

John 8:31–32

The grass withers, the flower fades, but the word of our God stands forever.

Isaiah 40:8

Man shall not live by bread alone, but by every word that proceeds from the mouth of God.

Matthew 4:4

Healing ❤

Call to Me, and I will answer you, and show you great and mighty things, which you do not know.

Jeremiah 33:3

Bless the LORD, O my soul,
And forget not all His benefits:
Who forgives all your iniquities,
Who heals all your diseases.

Psalm 103:2–3

Who Himself bore our sins in His own body on the tree, that we, having died to sins, might live for righteousness—by whose stripes you were healed.

1 Peter 2:24

Therefore we do not lose heart. Even though our outward man is perishing, yet the inward man is being renewed day by day. For our light affliction, which is but for a moment, is working for us a far more exceeding and eternal weight of glory.

2 Corinthians 4:16–17

The righteous cry out, and the LORD hears,
And delivers them out of all their troubles.
The LORD is near to those who have a
    broken heart,
And saves such as have a contrite spirit.
Many are the afflictions of the righteous,
But the LORD delivers him out of them all.
Psalm 34:17–19

The LORD God is my strength;
He will make my feet like deer's feet,
And He will make me walk on my high hills.
Habakkuk 3:19

My flesh and my heart fail;
But God is the strength of my heart and my
    portion forever.
Psalm 73:26

Turning Back to God

> I have loved you with an everlasting love;
>   Therefore with lovingkindness I have drawn
> you.
>
> *Jeremiah 31:3*

> Let the wicked forsake his way,
>   And the unrighteous man his thoughts;
>   Let him return to the LORD,
>   And He will have mercy on him;
>   And to our God,
>   For He will abundantly pardon.
>
> *Isaiah 55:7*

> If anyone cleanses himself . . . , he will be a
> vessel for honor, sanctified and useful for the
> Master, prepared for every good work.
>
> *2 Timothy 2:21*

> Draw near to God and He will draw near to
> you. Cleanse your hands, you sinners; and purify
> your hearts, you double-minded.
>
> *James 4:8*

> Put on the Lord Jesus Christ, and make no
> provision for the flesh, to fulfill its lusts.
>
> *Romans 13:14*

Now by this we know that we know Him, if we keep His commandments.

He who says, "I know Him," and does not keep His commandments, is a liar, and the truth is not in him.

But whoever keeps His word, truly the love of God is perfected in him. By this we know that we are in Him.

He who says he abides in Him ought himself also to walk just as He walked.

1 John 2:3–6

In Him we live and move and have our being, as also some of your own poets have said, "For we are also His offspring."

Acts 17:28

Blessed is the man who listens to me,
Watching daily at my gates,
Waiting at the posts of my doors.

Proverbs 8:34

As newborn babes, desire the pure milk of the word that you may grow thereby.

1 Peter 2:2

But be doers of the word, and not hearers only, deceiving yourselves.

James 1:22

Heaven—Your Home

This is the will of Him who sent Me, that everyone who sees the Son and believes in Him may have everlasting life; and I will raise him up at the last day.

John 6:40

The hope which is laid up for you in heaven, of which you heard before in the word of the truth of the gospel, which has come to you.

Colossians 1:5–6

Our citizenship is in heaven, from which we also eagerly wait for the Savior, the Lord Jesus Christ.

Philippians 3:20

For now we see in a mirror, dimly, but then face to face. Now I know in part, but then I shall know just as I also am known.

1 Corinthians 13:12

Assuredly, I say to you, I will no longer drink of the fruit of the vine until that day when I drink it new in the kingdom of God.

Mark 14:25

Surely goodness and mercy shall follow me all the days of my life; and I will dwell in the house of the LORD forever.

Psalm 23:6

God will wipe away every tear from their eyes; there shall be no more death, nor sorrow, nor crying. There shall be no more pain, for the former things have passed away.

Then He who sat on the throne said, "Behold, I make all things new." And He said to me, "Write, for these words are true and faithful."

And He said to me, "It is done! I am the Alpha and the Omega, the Beginning and the End. I will give of the fountain of the water of life freely to him who thirsts.

Revelation 21:4–6

Heavenly Rewards

Eye has not seen, nor ear heard, nor have entered into the heart of man the things which God has prepared for those who love Him.

1 Corinthians 2:9

Violence shall no longer be heard in your
    land,
Neither wasting nor destruction within your
    borders;
But you shall call your walls Salvation,
And your gates Praise.
The sun shall no longer be your light by day,
Nor for brightness shall the moon give light
    to you;
But the LORD will be to you an everlasting
    light,
And your God your glory.
Your sun shall no longer go down,
Nor shall your moon withdraw itself;
For the LORD will be your everlasting light,
And the days of your mourning shall be
    ended.

Isaiah 60:18–20

Those who are wise shall shine
Like the brightness of the firmament,
And those who turn many to righteousness
Like the stars forever and ever.

Daniel 12:3

For since the beginning of the world
Men have not heard nor perceived by the ear,
Nor has the eye seen any God besides You,
Who acts for the one who waits for Him.

Isaiah 64:4

He who sows righteousness will have a sure reward.

Proverbs 11:18

And behold, I am coming quickly, and My reward is with Me, to give to every one according to his work.

Revelation 22:12

Take heed that you do not do your charitable deeds before men, to be seen by them. Otherwise you have no reward from your Father in heaven.

Matthew 6:1

God will bring every work into judgment, including every secret thing, whether good or evil.

Ecclesiastes 12:14

Prayer 🖤

Be anxious for nothing, but in everything by prayer and supplication, with thanksgiving, let your requests be made known to God; and the peace of God, which surpasses all understanding, will guard your hearts and minds through Christ Jesus.

Philippians 4:6–7

Assuredly, I say to you, whatever you bind on earth will be bound in heaven, and whatever you loose on earth will be loosed in heaven.

Again I say to you that if two of you agree on earth concerning anything that they ask, it will be done for them by My Father in heaven.

Matthew 18:18–19

Let us therefore come boldly to the throne of grace, that we may obtain mercy and find grace to help in time of need.

Hebrews 4:16

Without faith it is impossible to please Him, for he who comes to God must believe that He is, and that He is a rewarder of those who diligently seek Him.

Hebrews 11:6

Confess your trespasses to one another, and pray for one another, that you may be healed. The effective, fervent prayer of a righteous man avails much.

James 5:16

LORD, I cry out to You;
Make haste to me!
Give ear to my voice when I cry out to You.
Let my prayer be set before You as incense,
The lifting up of my hands as the evening
    sacrifice.

Psalm 141:1–2

So I say to you, ask, and it will be given to you; seek, and you will find; knock, and it will be opened to you.

Luke 11:9

Then He spoke a parable to them, that men always ought to pray and not lose heart.

Luke 18:1

For the eyes of the LORD are on the righteous,
And His ears are open to their prayers;
But the face of the LORD is against those who do evil.

1 Peter 3:12

When you pray, you shall not be like the hypocrites. For they love to pray standing in the synagogues and on the corners of the streets, that they may be seen by men. Assuredly, I say to you, they have their reward.

But you, when you pray, go into your room, and when you have shut your door, pray to your Father who is in the secret place; and your Father who sees in secret will reward you openly.

Matthew 6:5–6

Evening and morning and at noon I will pray, and cry aloud, and He shall hear my voice.

Psalm 55:17

Christs Return

Looking for the blessed hope and glorious appearing of our great God and Savior Jesus Christ.

Titus 2:13

For this we say to you by the word of the Lord, that we who are alive and remain until the coming of the Lord will by no means precede those who are asleep.

For the Lord Himself will descend from heaven with a shout, with the voice of an archangel, and with the trumpet of God. And the dead in Christ will rise first.

Then we who are alive and remain shall be caught up together with them in the clouds to meet the Lord in the air. And thus we shall always be with the Lord.

Therefore comfort one another with these words.

1 Thessalonians 4:15–18

Who also said, "Men of Galilee, why do you stand gazing up into heaven? This same Jesus, who was taken up from you into heaven, will so come in like manner as you saw Him go into heaven."

Acts 1:11

Beloved, now we are children of God; and it has not yet been revealed what we shall be, but we know that when He is revealed, we shall be like Him, for we shall see Him as He is.

And everyone who has this hope in Him purifies himself, just as He is pure.

1 John 3:2–3

There is laid up for me the crown of righteousness, which the Lord, the righteous Judge, will give to me on that Day, and not to me only but also to all who have loved His appearing.

2 Timothy 4:8

And there will be signs in the sun, in the moon, and in the stars; and on the earth distress of nations, with perplexity, the sea and the waves roaring; men's hearts failing them from fear and the expectation of those things which are coming on the earth, for the powers of heaven will be shaken.

Then they will see the Son of Man coming in a cloud with power and great glory.

Now when these things begin to happen, look up and lift up your heads, because your redemption draws near.

Luke 21:25–28

Let not your heart be troubled; you believe in God, believe also in Me.

In My Father's house are many mansions; if it were not so, I would have told you. I go to prepare a place for you.

And if I go and prepare a place for you, I will come again and receive you to Myself; that where I am, there you may be also.

And where I go you know, and the way you know.

John 14:1–4

God's Goals for
Couples

Compassion

All of you be of one mind, having compassion for one another; love as brothers, be tenderhearted, be courteous.

1 Peter 3:8

He who finds his life will lose it, and he who loses his life for My sake will find it.

Matthew 10:39

He who has pity on the poor lends to the LORD, And He will pay back what he has given.

Proverbs 19:17

By this all will know that you are My disciples, if you have love for one another.

John 13:35

And whatever you do, do it heartily, as to the Lord and not to men, knowing that from the Lord you will receive the reward of the inheritance; for you serve the Lord Christ.

But he who does wrong will be repaid for what he has done, and there is no partiality.

Colossians 3:23–25

For we do not preach ourselves, but Christ Jesus the Lord, and ourselves your bondservants for Jesus' sake.

For it is the God who commanded light to shine out of darkness, who has shone in our hearts to give the light of the knowledge of the glory of God in the face of Jesus Christ.

But we have this treasure in earthen vessels, that the excellence of the power may be of God and not of us.

2 Corinthians 4:5–7

So the people asked him, saying, "What shall we do then?"

He answered and said to them, "He who has two tunics, let him give to him who has none; and he who has food, let him do likewise."

Luke 3:10–11

Command those who are rich in this present age not to be haughty, nor to trust in uncertain riches but in the living God, who gives us richly all things to enjoy.

Let them do good, that they be rich in good works, ready to give, willing to share, storing up for themselves a good foundation for the time to come, that they may lay hold on eternal life.

1 Timothy 6:17–19

Committment

Whatever you do, do it heartily, as to the Lord and not to men, knowing that from the Lord you will receive the reward of the inheritance; for you serve the Lord Christ.

Colossians 3:23–24

Being confident of this very thing, that He who has begun a good work in you will complete it until the day of Jesus Christ.

Philippians 1:6

Let us not grow weary while doing good, for in due season we shall reap if we do not lose heart.

Galatians 6:9

You did not choose Me, but I chose you and appointed you that you should go and bear fruit, and that your fruit should remain, that whatever you ask the Father in My name He may give you.

These things I command you, that you love one another.

John 15:16–17

When He had called the people to Himself, with His disciples also, He said to them, "Whoever desires to come after Me, let him deny himself, and take up his cross, and follow Me.

"For whoever desires to save his life will lose it, but whoever loses his life for My sake and the gospel's will save it.

"For what will it profit a man if he gains the whole world, and loses his own soul?

"Or what will a man give in exchange for his soul?"

Mark 8:34–37

When you make a vow to God, do not delay to pay it; for He has no pleasure in fools. Pay what you have vowed- Better not to vow than to vow and not pay.

Ecclesiastes 5:4-5

Then Jesus said to His disciples, "If anyone desires to come after Me, let him deny himself, and take up his cross, and follow Me."

Matthew 16:24

Contentment

We know that all things work together for good to those who love God, to those who are the called according to His purpose.

Romans 8:28

Let your conduct be without covetousness; be content with such things as you have. For He Himself has said, "I will never leave you nor forsake you." So we may boldly say: "The LORD is my helper; I will not fear. What can man do to me?"

Hebrews 13:5–6

Delight yourself also in the LORD, and He shall give you the desires of your heart.

Psalm 37:4

Now godliness with contentment is great gain.
For we brought nothing into this world, and it is certain we can carry nothing out.
And having food and clothing, with these we shall be content.

1 Timothy 6:6–8

"Therefore do not worry, saying, 'What shall we eat?' or 'What shall we drink?' or 'What shall we wear?'

"For after all these things the Gentiles seek. For your heavenly Father knows that you need all these things.

"But seek first the kingdom of God and His righteousness, and all these things shall be added to you.

"Therefore do not worry about tomorrow, for tomorrow will worry about its own things. Sufficient for the day is its own trouble."

Matthew 6:31–34

Be anxious for nothing, but in everything by prayer and supplication, with thanksgiving, let your requests be made known to God; and the peace of God, which surpasses all understanding, will guard your hearts and minds through Christ Jesus.

Not that I speak in regard to need, for I have learned in whatever state I am, to be content: I know how to be abased, and I know how to abound. Everywhere and in all things I have learned both to be full and to be hungry, both to abound and to suffer need.

I can do all things through Christ who strengthens me.

Philippians 4:6, 7, 11–13

Endurance

Blessed is the man who endures temptation; for when he has been approved, he will receive the crown of life which the Lord has promised to those who love Him. Therefore submit to God. Resist the devil and he will flee from you.

James 1:12; 4:7

But He knows the way that I take;
When He has tested me, I shall come forth as gold.

Job 23:10

If anyone serves Me, let him follow Me; and where I am, there My servant will be also. If anyone serves Me, him My Father will honor.

John 12:26

To be carnally minded is death, but to be spiritually minded is life and peace.

Romans 8:6

Abide in Me, and I in you. As the branch cannot bear fruit of itself, unless it abides in the vine, neither can you, unless you abide in Me.

I am the vine, you are the branches. He who abides in Me, and I in him, bears much fruit; for without Me you can do nothing.

John 15:4–5

He who dwells in the secret place of the
    Most High
Shall abide under the shadow of the Almighty.
I will say of the LORD, "He is my refuge and
    my fortress;
My God, in Him I will trust."

Psalm 91:1–2

The LORD upholds all who fall,
And raises up all who are bowed down.
The eyes of all look expectantly to You,
And You give them their food in due season.
You open Your hand
And satisfy the desire of every living thing.

Psalm 145:14–16

Forgiveness ❤️

Let all bitterness, wrath, anger, clamor, and evil speaking be put away from you, with all malice. And be kind to one another, tenderhearted, forgiving one another, just as God in Christ forgave you.

Ephesians 4:31–32

Judge not, and you shall not be judged. Condemn not, and you shall not be condemned. Forgive, and you will be forgiven.

Luke 6:37

If you forgive men their trespasses, your heavenly Father will also forgive you.

But if you do not forgive men their trespasses, neither will your Father forgive your trespasses.

Matthew 6:14–15

Then Peter came to Him and said, "Lord, how often shall my brother sin against me, and I forgive him? Up to seven times?"

Jesus said to him, "I do not say to you, up to seven times, but up to seventy times seven."

Matthew 18:21–22

Take heed to yourselves. If your brother sins against you, rebuke him; and if he repents, forgive him.

Luke 17:3

Whenever you stand praying, if you have anything against anyone, forgive him, that your Father in heaven may also forgive you your trespasses.

Mark 11:25

Bearing with one another, and forgiving one another, if anyone has a complaint against another; even as Christ forgave you, so you also must do.

Colossians 3:13

Blessed are those who are persecuted for righteousness' sake, for theirs is the kingdom of heaven.

Blessed are you when they revile and persecute you, and say all kinds of evil against you falsely for My sake.

Rejoice and be exceedingly glad, for great is your reward in heaven, for so they persecuted the prophets who were before you.

Matthew 5:10–12

Generosity 🖤

He who has a generous eye will be blessed, for he gives of his bread to the poor.

Proverbs 22:9

Give, and it will be given to you: good measure, pressed down, shaken together, and running over will be put into your bosom. For with the same measure that you use, it will be measured back to you."

Luke 6:38

Honor the LORD with your possessions,
And with the firstfruits of all your increase;
So your barns will be filled with plenty,
And your vats will overflow with new wine.

Proverbs 3:9–10

The generous soul will be made rich,
And he who waters will also be watered himself.

Proverbs 11:25

He who sows sparingly will also reap sparingly, and he who sows bountifully will also reap bountifully.

So let each one give as he purposes in his heart, not grudgingly or of necessity; for God loves a cheerful giver.

2 Corinthians 9:6–7

He who is faithful in what is least is faithful also in much; and he who is unjust in what is least is unjust also in much.

Therefore if you have not been faithful in the unrighteous mammon, who will commit to your trust the true riches?

Luke 16:10–11

Does he thank that servant because he did the things that were commanded him? I think not.

So likewise you, when you have done all those things which you are commanded, say, "We are unprofitable servants. We have done what was our duty to do."

Luke 17:9–10

Do not lay up for yourselves treasures on earth, where moth and rust destroy and where thieves break in and steal; but lay up for yourselves treasures in heaven, where neither moth nor rust destroys and where thieves do not break in and steal.

For where your treasure is, there your heart will be also.

Matthew 6:19–21

Give to the LORD the glory due His name; bring an offering, and come into His courts.

Psalm 96:8

Honesty 🖤

In mercy and truth
Atonement is provided for iniquity;
And by the fear of the LORD one departs
from evil.

Proverbs 16:6

The truthful lip shall be established forever,
But a lying tongue is but for a moment.

Proverbs 12:19

Therefore, putting away lying, "Let each one
of you speak truth with his neighbor," for we are
members of one another.

Ephesians 4:25

Let no corrupt word proceed out of your
mouth, but what is good for necessary edification,
that it may impart grace to the hearers.

Let all bitterness, wrath, anger, clamor, and
evil speaking be put away from you, with all malice.

And be kind to one another, tenderhearted,
forgiving one another, just as God in Christ forgave you.

Ephesians 4:29, 31–32

Pleasant words are like a honeycomb, Sweetness to the soul and health to the bones.

Proverbs 16:24

He who guards his mouth preserves his life, But he who opens wide his lips shall have destruction.

Proverbs 13:3

A good man out of the good treasure of his heart brings forth good; and an evil man out of the evil treasure of his heart brings forth evil. For out of the abundance of the heart his mouth speaks.

Luke 6:45

Whoever guards his mouth and tongue keeps his soul from troubles.

Proverbs 21:23

Death and life are in the power of the tongue, and those who love it will eat its fruit.

Proverbs 18:21

Humility

> Whoever humbles himself as this little child is the greatest in the kingdom of heaven.
>
> *Matthew 18:4*

> I will praise the name of God with a song,
> And will magnify Him with thanksgiving.
> This also shall please the LORD better than
>   an ox or bull,
> Which has horns and hooves.
> The humble shall see this and be glad;
> And you who seek God, your hearts shall
>   live.
>
> *Psalm 69:30–32*

> Who is wise and understanding among you? Let him show by good conduct that his works are done in the meekness of wisdom.
>
> *James 3:13*

> But we have this treasure in earthen vessels, that the excellence of the power may be of God and not of us.
>
> *2 Corinthians 4:7*

Pride goes before destruction,
And a haughty spirit before a fall.
Better to be of a humble spirit with the lowly,
Than to divide the spoil with the proud.
He who heeds the word wisely will find
good,
And whoever trusts in the LORD, happy is he.

Proverbs 16:18–20

He who is of a proud heart stirs up strife,
But he who trusts in the LORD will be pros-
pered.
He who trusts in his own heart is a fool,
But whoever walks wisely will be delivered.

Proverbs 28:25–26

Yet it shall not be so among you; but whoever desires to become great among you, let him be your servant
And whoever desires to be first among you, let him be your slave.

Matthew 20:26–27

But He gives more grace. Therefore He says: "God resists the proud, but gives grace to the humble."
Therefore submit to God. Resist the devil and he will flee from you.
Humble yourselves in the sight of the Lord, and He will lift you up.

James 4:6–7, 10

Likewise you younger people, submit yourselves to your elders. Yes, all of you be submissive to one another, and be clothed with humility, for "God resists the proud, but gives grace to the humble."

Therefore humble yourselves under the mighty hand of God, that He may exalt you in due time.

1 Peter 5:5–6

Take My yoke upon you and learn from Me, for I am gentle and lowly in heart, and you will find rest for your souls.

For My yoke is easy and My burden is light.

Matthew 11:29–30

The fear of the LORD is the instruction of wisdom, and before honor is humility.

Proverbs 15:33

Love 🖤

Let love be without hypocrisy. Abhor what is evil. Cling to what is good. Be kindly affectionate to one another with brotherly love, in honor giving preference to one another.

Romans 12:9–10

Therefore be imitators of God as dear children. And walk in love, as Christ also has loved us and given Himself for us, an offering and a sacrifice to God for a sweet-smelling aroma.

Ephesians 5:1–2

Above all these things put on love, which is the bond of perfection.

Colossians 3:14

And we have known and believed the love that God has for us. God is love, and he who abides in love abides in God, and God in him.
We love Him because He first loved us.

1 John 4:16, 19

I love those who love me, and those who seek me diligently will find me.

Proverbs 8:17

Beloved, let us love one another, for love is of God; and everyone who loves is born of God and knows God.

He who does not love does not know God, for God is love.

In this the love of God was manifested toward us, that God has sent His only begotten Son into the world, that we might live through Him.

In this is love, not that we loved God, but that He loved us and sent His Son to be the propitiation for our sins.

Beloved, if God so loved us, we also ought to love one another.

No one has seen God at any time. If we love one another, God abides in us, and His love has been perfected in us.

1 John 4:7–12

He who has My commandments and keeps them, it is he who loves Me. And he who loves Me will be loved by My Father, and I will love him and manifest Myself to him.

John 14:21

As the Father loved Me, I also have loved you; abide in My love.

If you keep My commandments, you will abide in My love, just as I have kept My Father's commandments and abide in His love.

These things I have spoken to you, that My joy may remain in you, and that your joy may be full.

This is My commandment, that you love one another as I have loved you.

Greater love has no one than this, than to lay down one's life for his friends.

These things I command you, that you love one another.

John 15:9–13, 17

Purity 🖤🖤

I say then: Walk in the Spirit, and you shall not fulfill the lust of the flesh.

Galatians 5:16

Delight yourself also in the LORD,
And He shall give you the desires of your
  heart.
Commit your way to the LORD,
Trust also in Him,
And He shall bring it to pass.

Psalm 37:4–5

Put off, concerning your former conduct, the old man which grows corrupt according to the deceitful lusts, and be renewed in the spirit of your mind, and that you put on the new man which was created according to God, in true righteousness and holiness.

Ephesians 4:22–24

But I discipline my body and bring it into subjection, lest, when I have preached to others, I myself should become disqualified.

1 Corinthians 9:27

That you may become blameless and harmless, children of God without fault in the midst of a crooked and perverse generation, among whom you shine as lights in the world, holding fast the word of life, so that I may rejoice in the day of Christ that I have not run in vain or labored in vain.

Philippians 2:15–16

As He who called you is holy, you also be holy in all your conduct.

1 Peter 1:15

He who would love life and see good days, let him refrain his tongue from evil, and his lips from speaking deceit.

1 Peter 3:10

Let no one despise your youth, but be an example to the believers in word, in conduct, in love, in spirit, in faith, in purity.

I Timothy 4:12

For the grace of God that brings salvation has appeared to all men, teaching us that, denying ungodliness and worldly lusts, we should live soberly, righteously, and godly in the present age, looking for the blessed hope and glorious appearing of our great God and Savior Jesus Christ.

Titus 2:11-13

Steadfastness ♥

He who believes in Me, as the Scripture has said, out of his heart will flow rivers of living water.

John 7:38

Blessed is the man who fears the LORD,
Who delights greatly in His commandments.

Psalm 112:1

I will instruct you and teach you in the way you should go;
I will guide you with My eye.

Psalm 32:8

Brethren, I do not count myself to have apprehended; but one thing I do, forgetting those things which are behind and reaching forward to those things which are ahead, I press toward the goal for the prize of the upward call of God in Christ Jesus.

Philippians 3:13–14

Blessed is the man who endures temptation; for when he has been approved, he will receive the crown of life which the Lord has promised to those who love Him.

James 1:12

As long as my breath is in me,
And the breath of God in my nostrils,
My lips will not speak wickedness,
Nor my tongue utter deceit.

Job 27:3–4

But He knows the way that I take;
When He has tested me, I shall come forth as
    gold.
My foot has held fast to His steps;
I have kept His way and not turned aside.

Job 23:10–11

For by You I can run against a troop,
By my God I can leap over a wall.
As for God, His way is perfect;
The word of the LORD is proven;
He is a shield to all who trust in Him.
It is God who arms me with strength,
And makes my way perfect.

Psalm 18:29–30, 32

Therefore, my beloved brethren, be steadfast, immovable, always abounding in the work of the Lord, knowing that your labor is not in vain in the Lord.

I Corinthians 15:58

Be sober, be vigilant; because your adversary the devil walks about like a roaring lion, seeking whom he may devour. Resist him, steadfast in the faith, knowing that the same sufferings are experienced by your brotherhood in the world.

I Peter 5:8-9

Thoughtfulness

But also for this very reason, giving all diligence, add to your faith virtue, to virtue knowledge, to knowledge self-control, to self-control perseverance, to perseverance godliness, to godliness brotherly kindness, and to brotherly kindness love.

2 Peter 1:5–7

Let no one seek his own, but each one the other's well-being.

1 Corinthians 10:24

I have shown you in every way, by laboring like this, that you must support the weak. And remember the words of the Lord Jesus, that He said, "It is more blessed to give than to receive."

Acts 20:35

Walk in love, as Christ also has loved us and given Himself for us, an offering and a sacrifice to God for a sweet-smelling aroma.

Ephesians 5:2

Now may the God of patience and comfort grant you to be like-minded toward one another, according to Christ Jesus, that you may with one mind and one mouth glorify the God and Father of our Lord Jesus Christ.

Therefore receive one another, just as Christ also received us, to the glory of God.

Romans 15:5–7

For where envy and self-seeking exist, confusion and every evil thing are there.

But the wisdom that is from above is first pure, then peaceable, gentle, willing to yield, full of mercy and good fruits, without partiality and without hypocrisy.

Now the fruit of righteousness is sown in peace by those who make peace.

James 3:16–18

God's Solutions for Couples

Anger

Let every man be swift to hear, slow to speak, slow to wrath; for the wrath of man does not produce the righteousness of God.

James 1:19–20

A soft answer turns away wrath, but a harsh word stirs up anger.

Proverbs 15:1

Not returning evil for evil or reviling for reviling, but on the contrary blessing, knowing that you were called to this, that you may inherit a blessing.

1 Peter 3:9

The wisdom that is from above is first pure, then peaceable, gentle, willing to yield, full of mercy and good fruits, without partiality and without hypocrisy. Now the fruit of righteousness is sown in peace by those who make peace.

James 3:17–18

Cease from anger, and forsake wrath;
Do not fret—*it* only *causes* harm.
For evildoers shall be cut off;
But those who wait on the LORD,
They shall inherit the earth.

Psalm 37:8–9

He who is slow to anger is better than the mighty, and he who rules his spirit than he who takes a city.

Proverbs 16:32

Discouragement

> I was vexed in my mind. . . .
> Nevertheless I am continually with You;
> You hold me by my right hand.
> You will guide me with Your counsel.
> *Psalm 73:21–24*

> God is not the author of confusion but of
> peace, as in all the churches of the saints.
> *1 Corinthians 14:33*

> I was sought by those who did not ask for
>   Me;
> I was found by those who did not seek Me.
> I said, "Here I am, here I am."
> *Isaiah 65:1*

> He is our God, and we are the people
> of His pasture, and the sheep of His hand.
> *Psalm 95:7*

> Wait on the LORD;
> be of good courage
> and He shall strengthen your heart.
> Wait, I say, on the LORD.
> *Psalm 27:14*

You are a chosen generation, a royal priesthood . . .

His own special people, that you may proclaim the praises of Him who called you out of darkness into His marvelous light.

1 Peter 2:9

Create in me a clean heart, O God,
And renew a steadfast spirit within me.
Do not cast me away from Your presence,
And do not take Your Holy Spirit from me.
Restore to me the joy of Your salvation,
And uphold me by Your generous Spirit.

Psalm 51:10–12

The LORD also will be a refuge for the
    oppressed,
A refuge in times of trouble.
And those who know Your name will put
    their trust in You;
For You, LORD, have not forsaken those who
    seek You.

Psalm 9:9–10

Who shall separate us from the love of Christ? Shall tribulation, or distress, or persecution, or famine, or nakedness, or peril, or sword? . . . Yet in all these things we are more than conquerors through Him who loved us.

Romans 8:35–37

Turn Yourself to me, and have mercy on me,
For I am desolate and afflicted.
The troubles of my heart have enlarged;
Bring me out of my distresses! . . .
Keep my soul and deliver me;
Let me not be ashamed, for I put my trust in
 You.

Psalm 25:16, 17, 20

Failure 🖤

I, the LORD your God, will hold your right hand,
Saying to you, 'Fear not, I will help you.'

Isaiah 41:13

Now may our Lord Jesus Christ Himself, and
our God and Father, who has loved us and given
us everlasting consolation and good hope by grace,
comfort your hearts and establish you in every
good word and work.

2 Thessalonians 2:16–17

I will lead them in paths they have not known.
I will make darkness light before them,
And crooked places straight.
These things I will do for them,
And not forsake them.

Isaiah 42:16

Why are you cast down, O my soul?
And why are you disquieted within me?
Hope in God;
For I shall yet praise Him,
The help of my countenance and my God.

Psalm 42:11

I will be glad and rejoice in Your mercy,
For You have considered my trouble;
You have known my soul in adversities,

Psalm 31:7

The LORD is good,
A stronghold in the day of trouble;
And He knows those who trust in Him.

Nahum 1:7

Financial Troubles

My God shall supply all your need according to His riches in glory by Christ Jesus.

Philippians 4:19

The love of money is a root of all kinds of evil, for which some have strayed from the faith in their greediness, and pierced themselves through with many sorrows.

But you, O man of God, flee these things and pursue righteousness, godliness, faith, love, patience, gentleness.

1 Timothy 6:10–11

Trust in the LORD, and do good;
Dwell in the land, and feed on His faithfulness.
Delight yourself also in the LORD,
And He shall give you the desires of your heart.

Psalm 37:3–4

So we may boldly say: "The LORD is my helper; I will not fear. What can man do to me?"

Hebrews 13:6

He who trusts in his riches will fall, but the righteous will flourish like foliage.

Proverbs 11:28

Command those who are rich in this present age not to be haughty, nor to trust in uncertain riches but in the living God, who gives us richly all things to enjoy.

Let them do good, that they be rich in good works, ready to give, willing to share, storing up for themselves a good foundation for the time to come, that they may lay hold on eternal life.

1 Timothy 6:17–19

There is one who makes himself rich, yet has nothing; and one who makes himself poor, yet has great riches.

Wealth gained by dishonesty will be diminished, but he who gathers by labor will increase.

Proverbs 13:7, 11

Remove falsehood and lies far from me; give me neither poverty nor riches—feed me with the food allotted to me.

Proverbs 30:8

For you have need of endurance, so that after you have done the will of God, you may receive the promise:

Hebrews 10:36

Heartbreak 🖤

The Lord has anointed me . . .
To comfort all who mourn, . . .
To give them beauty for ashes,
The oil of joy for mourning.

Isaiah 61:1–2

He is despised and rejected by men,
A Man of sorrows and acquainted with grief.
And we hid, as it were, our faces from Him;
He was despised, and we did not esteem Him.

Isaiah 53:3

You have seen, for You observe trouble and
grief,
To repay it by Your hand.
The helpless commits himself to You;
You are the helper of the fatherless.

Psalm 10:14

Cast your burden on the LORD,
And He shall sustain you;
He shall never permit the righteous to be
moved.

Psalm 55:22

Those who sow in tears
Shall reap in joy.
He who continually goes forth weeping,
Bearing seed for sowing,
Shall doubtless come again with rejoicing,
Bringing his sheaves with him.

Psalm 126:5–6

The LORD has anointed Me
To preach good tidings to the poor;
He has sent Me to heal the brokenhearted.

Isaiah 61:1

But I say to you who hear: Love your enemies,
do good to those who hate you, "bless those who
curse you, and pray for those who spitefully use
you."

Luke 6:27–28

The LORD also will be a refuge for the oppressed,
A refuge in times of trouble.

Psalm 9:9

The Lord GOD will help Me;
Therefore I will not be disgraced;
Therefore I have set My face like a flint,
And I know that I will not be ashamed.

Isaiah 50:7

Sexual Impurity 🖤

Walk in the Spirit, and you shall not fulfill the lust of the flesh.

Galatians 5:16

No temptation has overtaken you except such as is common to man; but God is faithful, who will not allow you to be tempted beyond what you are able, but with the temptation will also make the way of escape, that you may be able to bear it.

1 Corinthians 10:13

Whoever commits sin is a slave of sin. And a slave does not abide in the house forever, but a son abides forever. Therefore if the Son makes you free, you shall be free indeed.

John 8:34–36

The Lord knows how to deliver the godly out of temptations and to reserve the unjust under punishment for the day of judgment.

2 Peter 2:9

Do you not know that your bodies are members of Christ? Shall I then take the members of Christ and make them members of a harlot? Certainly not!

Or do you not know that he who is joined to a harlot is one body with her? For "the two," He says, "shall become one flesh."

But he who is joined to the Lord is one spirit with Him.

Flee sexual immorality. Every sin that a man does is outside the body, but he who

commits sexual immorality sins against his own body.

Or do you not know that your body is the temple of the Holy Spirit who is in you, whom you have from God, and you are not your own?

For you were bought at a price; therefore glorify God in your body and in your spirit, which are God's.

1 Corinthians 6:15–20

I say then: Walk in the Spirit, and you shall not fulfill the lust of the flesh.

For the flesh lusts against the Spirit, and the Spirit against the flesh; and these are contrary to one another, so that you do not do the things that you wish.

Galatians 5:16–17

Put off, concerning your former conduct, the old man which grows corrupt according to the deceitful lusts, and be renewed in the spirit of your mind, and . . . put on the new man which was created according to God, in true righteousness and holiness . . . nor give place to the devil.

Ephesians 4:22–24, 27

Now therefore, listen to me, my children;
Pay attention to the words of my mouth:
Do not let your heart turn aside to her ways,
Do not stray into her paths;
For she has cast down many wounded,
And all who were slain by her were strong
    men.
Her house is the way to hell,
Descending to the chambers of death.

Proverbs 7:24–27

My brethren, count it all joy when you fall into various trials, knowing that the testing of your faith produces patience.

But let patience have its perfect work, that you may be perfect and complete, lacking nothing.

James 1:2–4

Do not lust after her beauty in your heart,
Nor let her allure you with her eyelids.
For by means of a harlot
A man is reduced to a crust of bread;
And an adulteress will prey upon his precious
life.

Proverbs 6:25–26

Stress 💕

Be strong and of good courage, do not fear nor be afraid of them; for the LORD your God, He is the One who goes with you. He will not leave you nor forsake you.

Deuteronomy 31:6

Peace I leave with you, My peace I give to you; not as the world gives do I give to you. Let not your heart be troubled, neither let it be afraid.

John 14:27

The LORD is near to all who call upon Him,
To all who call upon Him in truth.
He will fulfill the desire of those who fear Him;
He also will hear their cry and save them.

Psalm 145:18–19

Be anxious for nothing, but in everything by prayer and supplication, with thanksgiving, let your requests be made known to God; and the peace of God, which surpasses all understanding, will guard your hearts and minds through Christ Jesus.

Philippians 4:6–7

You will keep him in perfect peace, whose mind is stayed on You, because he trusts in You.

Isaiah 26:3

May the God of hope fill you with all joy and peace in believing, that you may abound in hope by the power of the Holy Spirit.

Romans 15:13

Temptation 🖤🖤

Blessed is the man who endures temptation; for when he has been approved, he will receive the crown of life which the Lord has promised to those who love Him.

James 1:12

The Lord knows how to deliver the godly out of temptations and to reserve the unjust under punishment for the day of judgment.

2 Peter 2:9

No temptation has overtaken you except such as is common to man; but God is faithful, who will not allow you to be tempted beyond what you are able, but with the temptation will also make the way of escape, that you may be able to bear it.

1 Corinthians 10:13

He has redeemed my soul in peace from the battle that was against me, for there were many against me.

Psalm 55:18

Now the Lord is the Spirit; and where the Spirit of the Lord is, there is liberty.

2 Corinthians 3:17

And you shall know the truth, and the truth shall make you free. Therefore if the Son makes you free, you shall be free indeed.

John 8:32, 36

Therefore submit to God. Resist the devil and he will flee from you.

James 4:7

Keep your heart with all diligence,
For out of it spring the issues of life.
Put away from you a deceitful mouth,
And put perverse lips far from you.
Let your eyes look straight ahead,
And your eyelids look right before you.
Ponder the path of your feet,
And let all your ways be established.
Do not turn to the right or the left;
Remove your foot from evil.

Proverbs 4:23–27

Obey My voice, and I will be your God, and you shall be My people. And walk in all the ways that I have commanded you, that it may be well with you.

Jeremiah 7:23

Worry ♥♥

In righteousness you shall be established;
You shall be far from oppression, for you
    shall not fear;
And from terror, for it shall not come near
    you.

Isaiah 54:14

You have also given me the shield of Your sal-
    vation;
Your right hand has held me up,
Your gentleness has made me great.
You enlarged my path under me,
So my feet did not slip.

Psalm 18:35–36

He who dwells in the secret place of the Most
    High
Shall abide under the shadow of the Almighty.

Psalm 91:1

No weapon formed against you shall prosper,
And every tongue which rises against you in
    judgment.

Isaiah 54:17

But whoever listens to me will dwell safely,
And will be secure, without fear of evil.

Proverbs 1:33

He has delivered us from the power of darkness and conveyed us into the kingdom of the Son of His love.

Colossians 1:13

The Lord will deliver me from every evil work and preserve me for His heavenly kingdom. To Him be glory forever and ever.

2 Timothy 4:18

Rest in the Lord, and wait patiently for Him. Those who wait on the Lord, They shall inherit the earth.

Psalm 37:7,9

My flesh and my heart fail; but God is the strength of my heart and my portion forever.

Psalm 73:26

Worldly Influences

Do not imitate what is evil, but what is good,
He who does good is of God.

3 John 11

Be strong and of good courage; do not be afraid,
   nor be dismayed, for the LORD your God
   is with you wherever you go.

Joshua 1:9

Those who trust in the LORD
Are like Mount Zion,
Which cannot be moved, but abides forever.
Do good, O LORD, to those who are good,
And to those who are upright in their hearts.

Psalm 125:1, 4

If anyone desires to come after Me, let him deny himself, and take up his cross daily, and follow Me. For whoever desires to save his life will lose it, but whoever loses his life for My sake will save it.

Luke 9:23–24

If we endure,
We shall also reign with Him.
If we deny Him,
He also will deny us.
If we are faithless,
He remains faithful;
He cannot deny Himself.

2 Timothy 2:11–13

Let us not grow weary while doing good, for in due season we shall reap if we do not lose heart.

Galatians 6:9

God's Blessings for Couples

Abundant Good

For the LORD God is a sun and shield;
The LORD will give grace and glory;
No good thing will He withhold
From those who walk uprightly.

Psalm 84:11

He will bless those who fear the LORD,
Both small and great.

Psalm 115:13

God is able to make all grace abound toward you, that you, always having all sufficiency in all things, may have an abundance for every good work.

2 Corinthians 9:8

The eyes of the LORD run to and fro throughout the whole earth, to show Himself strong on behalf of those whose heart is loyal to Him.

2 Chronicles 16:9

The LORD your God, who goes before you, He will fight for you, according to all He did for you in Egypt before your eyes.

Deuteronomy 1:30

But the Lord is faithful, who will establish you and guard you from the evil one.

2 Thessalonians 3:3

Great is the LORD, and greatly to be praised;
And His greatness is unsearchable.
One generation shall praise Your works to another,
And shall declare Your mighty acts.
Your kingdom is an everlasting kingdom,
And Your dominion endures throughout all generations.

Psalm 145:3–4, 13

Divine Intervention

It shall come to pass
That before they call, I will answer;
And while they are still speaking, I will hear.

Isaiah 65:24

Oh, sing to the LORD a new song!
For He has done marvelous things;
His right hand and His holy arm have gained
    Him the victory.

Psalm 98:1

If My people who are called by My name will
humble themselves, and pray and seek My face,
and turn from their wicked ways, then I will hear
from heaven, and will forgive their sin and heal
their land.

2 Chronicles 7:14

Be thankful to Him, and bless His name.
For the LORD is good;
His mercy is everlasting,
And His truth endures to all generations.

Psalm 100:4–5

To Him who is able to do exceedingly abundantly above all that we ask or think, according to the power that works in us, to Him be glory . . . forever and ever.

Ephesians 3:20–21

I would have lost heart, unless I had believed
That I would see the goodness of the LORD
In the land of the living.

Psalm 27:13

Gifts ❤❤

As each one has received a gift, minister it to one another, as good stewards of the manifold grace of God.

1 Peter 4:10

There are diversities of gifts, but the same Spirit. There are differences of ministries, but the same Lord.

1 Corinthians 12:4–5

Every good gift and every perfect gift is from above, and comes down from the Father of lights, with whom there is no variation or shadow of turning.

James 1:17

God's Faithfulness

He Himself has said, "I will never leave you nor forsake you."

Hebrews 13:5

The LORD will give strength to His people;
The LORD will bless His people with peace.

Psalm 29:11

God is faithful, by whom you were called into the fellowship of His Son, Jesus Christ our Lord.

1 Corinthians 1:9

Lo, I am with you always, even to the end of the age." Amen.

Matthew 28:20

His compassions fail not,
They are new every morning;
Great is Your faithfulness.

Lamentations 3:22–23

"Am I a God near at hand," says the LORD,
"And not a God afar off?
Can anyone hide himself in secret places,
So I shall not see him?" says the LORD;
"Do I not fill heaven and earth?" says the
    LORD.

Jeremiah 23:23–24

All nations before Him are as nothing,
And they are counted by Him less than noth-
    ing and worthless.
To whom then will you liken God?
Or what likeness will you compare to Him?
"To whom then will you liken Me,
Or to whom shall I be equal?" says the Holy
    One.
 Lift up your eyes on high,
And see who has created these things,
Who brings out their host by number;
He calls them all by name,
By the greatness of His might
And the strength of His power;
Not one is missing.
Have you not known?
Have you not heard?
The everlasting God, the LORD,
The Creator of the ends of the earth,
Neither faints nor is weary.
His understanding is unsearchable.

Isaiah 40:17, 18, 25, 26, 28

God's Friendship

You are My friends if you do whatever I command you.

No longer do I call you servants, for a servant does not know what his master is doing; but I have called you friends, for all things that I heard from My Father I have made known to you.

You did not choose Me, but I chose you and appointed you that you should go and bear fruit, and that your fruit should remain, that whatever you ask the Father in My name He may give you.

John 15:14–16

The LORD executes righteousness
And justice for all who are oppressed.

Psalm 103:6

The angel of the LORD encamps all around those who fear Him, and delivers them.

Psalm 34:7

And I have put My words in your mouth;
I have covered you with the shadow of My hand.

Isaiah 51:16

The heavens declare the glory of God; and the firmament shows His handiwork.

Psalm 19:1

Behold, I am the LORD, the God of all flesh. Is there anything too hard for Me?

Jeremiah 32:27

Whom have I in heaven but You? And there is none upon earth that I desire besides You.

Psalm 73:25

If we live, we live to the Lord; and if we die, we die to the Lord. Therefore, whether we live or die, we are the Lord's.

Romans 14:8

If we say that we have fellowship with Him, and walk in darkness, we lie and do not practice the truth.

But if we walk in the light as He is in the light, we have fellowship with one another, and the blood of Jesus Christ His Son cleanses us from all sin.

1 John 1:5–7

God's Love 🖤

But God demonstrates His own love toward us, in that while we were still sinners, Christ died for us.

Romans 5:8

We love Him because He first loved us.

1 John 4:19

We have known and believed the love that God has for us. God is love, and he who abides in love abides in God, and God in him.

1 John 4:16

By this we know love, because He laid down His life for us. And we also ought to lay down our lives for the brethren.

1 John 3:16

Blessed is he whose transgression is forgiven, whose sin is covered.

Blessed is the man to whom the LORD does not impute iniquity, and in whose spirit there is no deceit.

Psalm 32:1–2

Having been set free from sin, and having become slaves of God, you have your fruit to holiness, and the end, everlasting life.

Romans 6:22

Jesus answered and said to him, "If anyone loves Me, he will keep My word; and My Father will love him, and We will come to him and make Our home with him."

John 14:23

Behold what manner of love the Father has bestowed on us, that we should be called children of God! Therefore the world does not know us, because it did not know Him.

1 John 3:1

God's Mercy 🖤

We do not have a High Priest who cannot sympathize with our weaknesses, but was in all points tempted as we are, yet without sin. Let us therefore come boldly to the throne of grace, that we may obtain mercy and find grace to help in time of need.

Hebrews 4:15–16

The LORD God is a sun and shield;
The LORD will give grace and glory;
No good thing will He withhold
From those who walk uprightly.

Psalm 84:11

He has not dealt with us according to our
    sins,
Nor punished us according to our iniquities.
For as the heavens are high above the earth,
So great is His mercy toward those who fear
    Him;

Psalm 103:10–11

But God, who is rich in mercy, because of His great love with which He loved us, even when we were dead in trespasses, made us alive together with Christ (by grace you have been saved).

Ephesians 2:4–5

He saved them for His name's sake, that He might make His mighty power known.

Psalm 106:8

You have forgiven the iniquity of Your people;
You have covered all their sin. Selah

Psalm 85:2

As far as the east is from the west,
So far has He removed our transgressions
    from us.

Psalm 103:12

Commit your way to the LORD,
Trust also in Him,
And He shall bring it to pass.
He shall bring forth your righteousness as
    the light,
And your justice as the noonday.
Rest in the LORD, and wait patiently for
    Him;
Do not fret because of him who prospers in
    his way,
Because of the man who brings wicked schemes
    to pass.

Psalm 37:5–7

God's Rest 🖤

There remains therefore a rest for the people of God.

Let us therefore be diligent to enter that rest, lest anyone fall according to the same example of disobedience.

Seeing then that we have a great High Priest who has passed through the heavens, Jesus the Son of God, let us hold fast our confession.

Hebrews 4:9, 11, 14

He said, "My Presence will go with you, and I will give you rest."

Exodus 33:14

Therefore, having been justified by faith, we have peace with God through our Lord Jesus Christ, through whom also we have access by faith into this grace in which we stand, and rejoice in hope of the glory of God.

Romans 5:1–2

We know that all things work together for good to those who love God, to those who are the called according to His purpose.

Romans 8:28

God is not the author of confusion but of peace, as in all the churches of the saints.

1 Corinthians 14:33

Cast your burden on the LORD, and He shall sustain you; He shall never permit the righteous to be moved.

Psalm 55:22

The fear of man brings a snare, but whoever trusts in the LORD shall be safe.

Proverbs 29:25

Come to Me, all you who labor and hare heavy laden, and I will give you rest.

Matthew 11:28

Prayer Journal

_____

_____

_____

_____

_____

_____

_____

_____

_____

_____

_____

_____

_____

_____

_____

_____

Notes

Prayer Journal

_____

_____

_____

_____

_____

_____

_____

_____

_____

_____

_____

_____

_____

_____

_____

_____

Notes

Prayer Journal

_____

_____

_____

_____

_____

_____

_____

_____

_____

_____

_____

_____

_____

_____

_____

_____

_____

_____